RAINY DAY
Golf Games

by Edith Reiter an[d]

THE RAINY DAY GOLF[...]F
THE RAINY DAY COUNTRY CLUB

Enter the maze here to get to the club house

Published by Price/Stern/Sloan Publishers, Inc.
410 North La Cienega Boulevard, Los Angeles, California 90048

ISBN: 0-8431-1433-9

THE RAINY DAY GOLFER'S CROSSWORD PUZZLE

Use first names only to fill in the grid. We started you.

~~Slamming Sammy Snead~~
Isao Aoki
Tommy Armour
Andy Bean
Chip Beck
Gay Brewer
Rex Caldwell
Al Chandler
Jim Colbert
Charles Coody
Danny Edwards
Nick Faldo
Ed Fiori
Ron Funseth
Al Geiberger
Phil Hancock
Hale Irwin
Robert Jones
Tom Kite
Gene Littler
Larry Nelson
Jack Nicklaus
Arnie Palmer
Cal Peete
Henry Picard
Clarence Rose
Doug Sanders
J.C. Snead
Ed Sneed
Payne Stewart
Hal Sutton
Lee Trevino
Ken Venturi
Tom Watson

RAINY DAY COUNTRY CLUB
TWOSOME TOURNEY

Chip in the double letter to finish the words...

1. Pu____er
2. Chi____er
3. Sp____n
4. Umbre____a
5. Gi____ie
6. Bra____ie
7. Whi____
8. T____
9. W____ds
10. Du____er
11. Gr____n
12. Wa____le 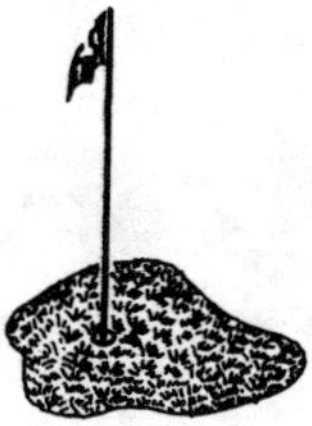  
13. H____k
14. Ca____away
15. Ca____ie
16. Ba____
17. Gra____
18. Ba____y
19. Scu____ing
20. O____onent
21. Handica____ing
22. Na____au 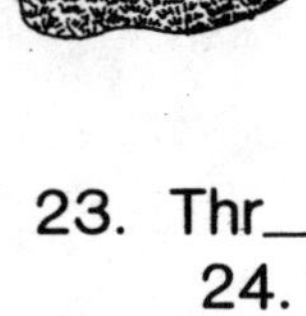
23. Thr____some
24. Gro____

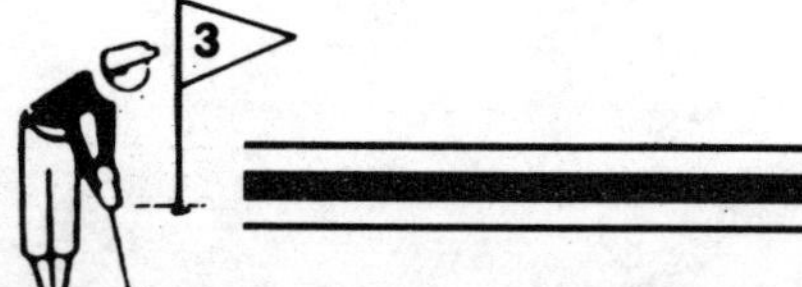

RAINY DAY COUNTRY CLUB OPEN

Unscramble the names on the LEADER BOARD.

ELE OVENRIT	____________
ARY YOLFD	____________
RYGA YRELAP	____________
CKIN DOLAF	____________
BEUHI EGNRE	____________
MTO TEIK	____________
NRALOD MAPLER	____________
DYNA NBAE	____________
LAC ETEEP	____________
KJAC CKALSINU	____________

OTHER FAMOUS COURSES

Match the golf course with its location.

1. Pebble Beach Golf Course	a. New Jersey
2. Winged Foot Golf Course	b. South Carolina
3. Augusta National Golf Course	c. Maryland
4. Colonial Country Club	d. Delaware
5. Pinehurst Country Club	e. Hawaii
6. Waialae Country Club	f. Ontario, Canada
7. Le Touquet	g. Pennsylvania
8. La Costa Country Club	h. Scotland
9. Hilton Head Island Country Club	i. Ireland
10. Glen Abbey Golf Course	j. So. California
11. Hershey Country Club	k. Florida
12. St. Andrews Golf Course	l. Ohio
13. Wilmington Country Club	m. England
14. Ballybunion Links	n. No. California
15. Doral Country Club	o. New York
16. Royal Liverpool	p. Arizona
17. Desert Highlands	q. France
18. Firestone Country Club	r. Georgia
19. Baltusrol Country Club	s. Texas
20. Congressional Country Club	t. North Carolina

THE RAINY DAY GOLFER'S "WHAT'S IN A NAME" TOURNAMENT

Fill in the blanks using some or all of the last names. We did one.

Clue	Answer	Name
1. Kind of nail	Pat Bradley	a. Tommy Armour
2. Meat dish		b. Pat Bradley
3. Instrument		c. Danny Edwards
4. Animal skin		d. Dale Eggeling
5. Month		e. Shirley Englehorn
6. Low		f. Ed Furgol
7. Wine		g. David Graham
8. Food		h. Phil Hancock
9. Rooster		i. George Mayer
10. Extremity		j. Cary Middlecoff
11. Hospital rooms		k. Orville Moody
12. Congestion		l. Payne Stewart
13. Breakfast food		m. Lee Trevino

RAINY DAY COUNTRY CLUB MID-WEEK TOURNEY

Unscramble the golf clothes. The circled letters spell a dangerous place at the RAINY DAY COUNTRY CLUB.

1. mooppsm
2. ebbrur talecs
3. lotwe

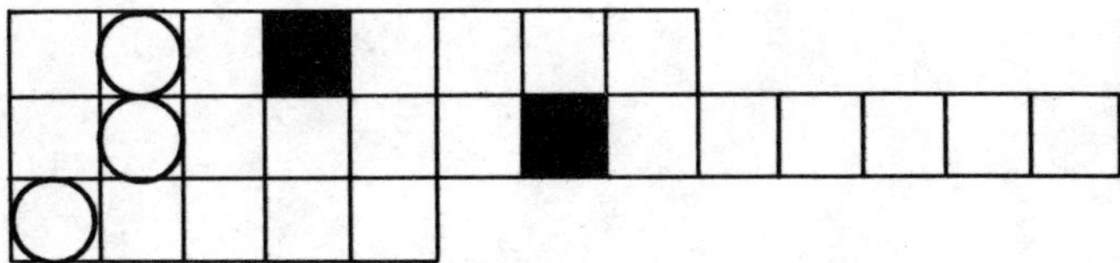

4. vloge
5. slup rusof

6. dniw karrebe
7. lyerag skosc
8. drumeba thossr
9. snu selagss
10. kepade pca
11. wtarese

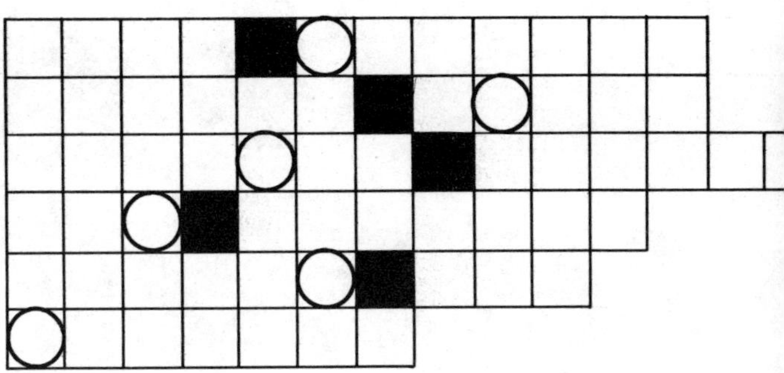

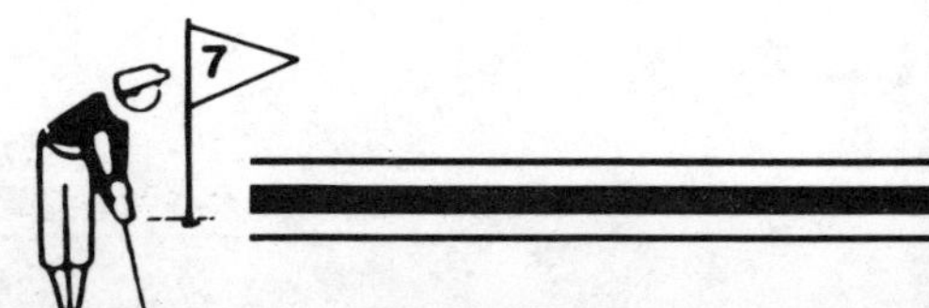

RAINY DAY GOLFER'S HALL OF FAME

WHO IS WHO?

1. Miller Barber	a) the dentist
2. Jo Anne Carner	b) the golden bear
3. Bruce Crampton	c) the white shark
4. Bing Crosby	d) the walrus
5. Walter Hagen	e) has an army
6. Ken Harrelson	f) big momma
7. Ben Hogan	g) the super Mex
8. Tony Lema	h) the babe
9. Cary Middlecoff	i) the eye doctor
10. Orville Moody	j) the hawk
11. Gil Morgan	k) the squire
12. Jack Nicklaus	l) the clam-bake-er
13. Greg Norman	m) the sarge
14. Arnie Palmer	n) Mr. X.
15. Gene Sarazen	o) little mouse
16. Craig Stadler	p) champagne Tony
17. Bob Toski	q) the iron man
18. Lee Trevino	r) bantam Ben
19. Mildred Zaharias	s) the Haig

RAINY DAY COUNTRY CLUB IS KNOWN FOR ITS ROUGH

Hiding in the rough are 27 golfers. Find their last names. Read crossways, upside down, sideway and backwards. Circle each name as you find it.

Isao AOKI
Tommy ARMOUR
Andy BEAN
Chip BECK
Patty BERG
Gay BREWER
George BURNS
T.C. CHEN
Bruce DEVLIN
Gardner DICKINSON
David EDWARDS
Dave EICHELBERGER
Lee ELDER
Hubie GREEN
Scott HOCH
Betsy KING
Wayne LEVI
Nancy LOPEZ
Mark LYE
Larry MIZE
Larry NELSON
Greg NORMAN
Sandra PALMER
Sandra POST
Jack RENNER
Laurie RINKER
Dan SIKES
Sam SNEAD

E	D	A	L	B	E	R	G	R	E	E	N
M	I	Z	E	R	E	L	A	S	V	P	O
Q	C	C	H	E	N	A	D	N	B	I	R
F	K	L	H	W	Q	S	N	E	A	D	M
H	I	E	C	E	S	H	C	L	R	E	A
O	N	V	T	R	L	K	C	S	Z	V	N
P	S	I	K	E	S	B	Z	O	L	L	R
A	O	K	I	N	G	U	E	N	H	I	E
L	N	S	V	N	P	R	P	R	E	N	K
M	A	M	T	E	V	N	O	Y	G	G	N
E	D	W	A	R	D	S	L	T	O	E	I
R	O	O	V	T	D	A	R	M	O	U	R

RAINY DAY COUNTRY CLUB
PRO SHOP - OLD TIMERS SALE

Match the early names with their modern counterparts.

1. Driving Iron	a. 1 wood
2. Cleek	b. 2 wood
3. Mashie Iron	c. 3 wood
4. Baffy	d. 4 wood
5. Pitcher	e. 5 wood
6. Mid-Mashie	f. 1 iron
7. Spoon	g. 2 iron
8. Mashie Niblick	h. 3 iron
9. Spade Mashie	i. 4 iron
10. Driver	j. 5 iron
11. Mid Iron	k. 6 iron
12. Brassie	l. 7 iron
13. Mashie	m. 8 iron
14. Niblick	n. 9 iron

THE RAINY DAY GOLFER'S PARAPHERNALIA

See how fast you can unscramble the list.

1. leur okob ____________________
2. otivd reprirae ____________________
3. tinscou pcu ____________________
4. yingt ____________________
5. ghas gab ____________________
6. grena drefni ____________________
7. nus ant oolnit ____________________
8. roecs urtocen ____________________
9. eltes srhub ____________________
10. cetsni lelepnter ____________________
11. ketcja ____________________
12. eshos ____________________
13. vlego ____________________
14. trupet ____________________
15. dnab-ida ____________________
16. prehicp ____________________
17. tha ____________________
18. blamrule ____________________
19. abll errmak ____________________
20. saxte deewg ____________________
21. heflwfi labl ____________________
22. dahe rosecv ____________________
23. blucs ____________________

RAINY DAY GOLFERS
would rather play golf...

1. than fly a ______________	a) Tommy ARMOUR
2. than drive a ______________	b) Miller BARBER
3. all year, not just in ______________	c) Gay BREWER
4. than be Sherlock's Dr. ______________	d) Al CHANDLER
5. than be Santa's red nosed ______________	e) John COOK
6. than climb a ______________	f) Lee ELDER
7. than ski up ______________	g) Doug FORD
8. than tramp through the ______________	h) Dave HILL
9. than work as a ______________	i) Barry JAECKEL
10. in "plus fours," than in ______________	j) Don JANUARY
11. than be a loving ______________	k) Tom KITE
12. than eat or ______________	l) Johnny MILLER
13. than be a church ______________	m) Jodie MUDD
14. than be a zebra or a ______________	n) Andy NORTH
15. than grind as a ______________	o) Clarence ROSE
16. than squish in the ______________	p) Mason RUDOLPH
17. than be a ship's ______________	q) Tommy VALENTINE
18. than be a red red ______________	r) Tom WATSON
19. than be a men's ______________	s) Craig WOODS

RAINY DAY COUNTRY CLUB PRO WANTS TO KNOW YOUR DISTANCE

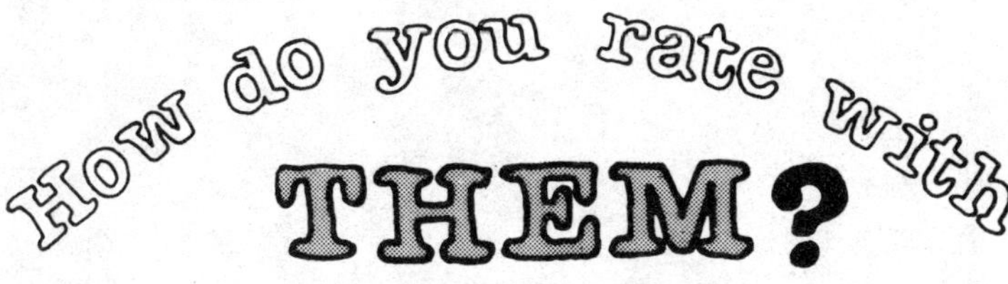

	AVERAGE MAN	AVERAGE WOMAN	YOUR DISTANCE
1 WOOD	220	190	______
2 WOOD	210	180	______
3 WOOD	200	170	______
4 WOOD	190	160	______
5 WOOD	180	150	______
1 IRON	190	160	______
2 IRON	180	150	______
3 IRON	170	140	______
4 IRON	160	130	______
5 IRON	150	120	______
6 IRON	140	110	______
7 IRON	130	100	______
8 IRON	120	90	______
9 IRON	110	80	______
PITCHING WEDGE	90	65	______
SAND WEDGE	70	50	______

RAINY DAY COUNTRY CLUB TRIVIA HANDICAP

1. Gene Sarazen is known for his:
   a. plus 2's
   b. plus 3's
   c. plus 4's
2. The first postage stamp relating to golf was issued in 1953 by:
   a. France
   b. Japan
   c. Great Britain

3. An Albatross is:
   a. 2 strokes under par
   b. 3 strokes under par
   c. a bird who loves to eat golfballs
4. Harry Vardon's "V" refers to his:
   a. style of grip
   b. type of sweater
   c. tour victories
5. The first "grand slam-er" was:
   a. Ben Hogan
   b. Bobby Jones
   c. Sam Snead
6. The American P.G.A. was founded in:
   a. 1906
   b. 1910
   c. 1916
7. If you are playing "Preferred Lies" you are:
   a. playing Winter rules
   b. playing Summer rules
   c. allowed to smooth out the sand

8. Crack is an old-fashioned term meaning:
   a. a good hit
   b. cutting the cover of the ball
   c. a first class golfer
9. When is the proper time to yell "fore?"
   a. before you hit
   b. after you hit

RAINY DAY COUNTRY CLUB
PRO-AM

Find the common last name of the Pros and Guests.

We did one.

1. Golfer and American author: Amy and Louisa May *Alcott*
2. Golfer and automobile manufacturer: Doug and Henry ________
3. Golfer and government administrator: Bobby and Jesse ________
4. Golfer and American poetess: Gardner and Emily ________
5. Golfer and movie mogul: Dick and Louis B. ________
6. Golfer and Sherlock's assistant: Tom and Dr. John ________
7. Golfer and Hollywood columnist: Lou and Sheila ________
8. Golfer and television personality: Betsy and Alan ________
9. Golfer and the duchess: Scott and Wallis B. ________
10. Golfer and bandleader: Johnny and Glenn ________
11. Golfer and American novelist: Rex and Erskine ________
12. Golfer and Hollywood star: Kathy and Brian ________
13. Golfer and opera singer: Tony and Beverly ________
14. Golfer and early pilot: Mickey and Orville ________
15. Golfer and Hollywood star: Jim and Claudette ________
16. Golfer and comedy band leader: Larry and Ozzie ________
17. Golfer and movie star: Donna and Loretta ________
18. Golfer and television commentator: Jodie and Roger ________
19. Golfer and silent screen star: Donna and Pearl ________
20. Golfer and movie star: Payne and James ________

RAINY DAY COUNTRY CLUB - FUN

WHICH CATEGORY DO YOU FIT?

1. What you should replace.
2. Not lifting feet on green.
3. Hitting before you should.
4. What's a swing and a miss?
5. Never do this when someone is swinging.
6. Never tee off in front of ______ .
7. Aiming one way and the ball goes the other way.

1. [_] _ _ _ _
2. _ _ [_] _ _
3. _ _ _ _ [_] _ _ _ _
4. _ _ _ [_] _
5. _ _ [_] _ _
6. _ _ [_] _ _ _ _
7. [_] _ _ _ _

1. What you wear.
2. One over par.
3. The ball goes right.
4. What you can yell on the course.
5. Two below par.
6. What you want to keep out of.
7. What you hope every putt will do.

1. [_] _ _ _ _
2. _ [_] _ _ _
3. _ [_] _ _ _
4. [_] _ _ _
5. [_] _ _ _ _
6. [_] _ _ _ _
7. [_] _ _ _

FIND THE ONLY SLEEVE*

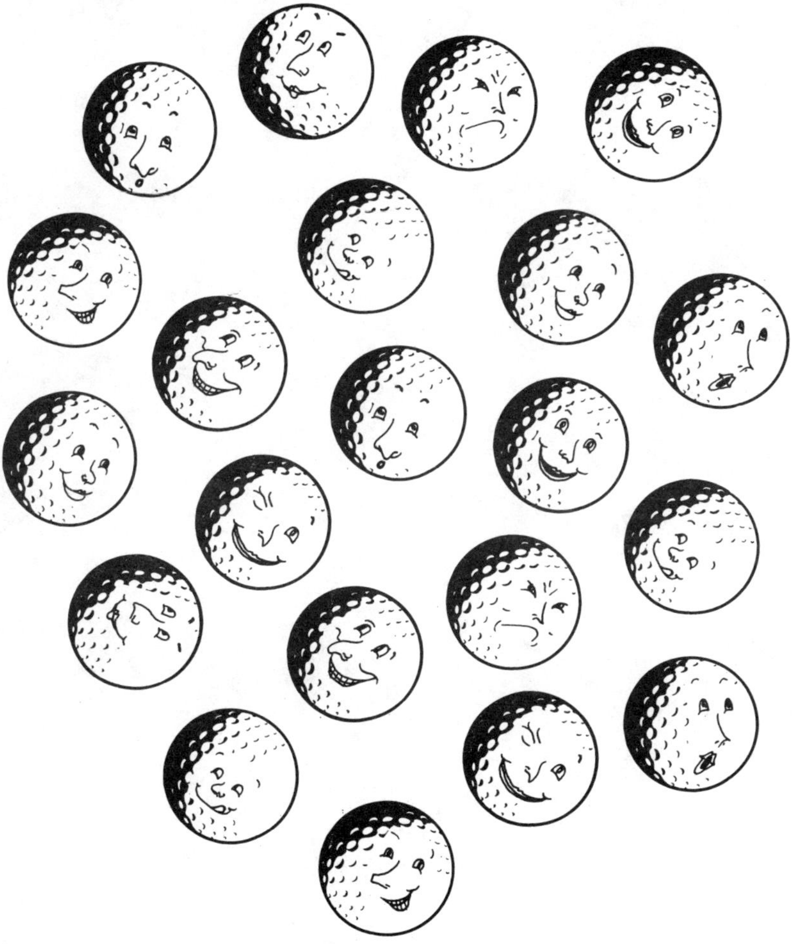

*That means three of a kind.

THE RAINY DAY COUNTRY CLUB SHOTGUN TOURNAMENT

Field the players, first names only.

AMY Alcott
LAURA Baugh
SUE Berning
CLIFFORD (Ann) Creed
FAY Crocker
ANN Dana
MARY (Lena) Faulk
MARLENE Hagge
BEVERLY Hanson
RUTH Jesson
MURLE Lindstrom
~~NANCY Lopez~~
ADA Mackenzie
SANDRA Palmer
HELEN Payson
JACKIE Pung
JUDY Rankin
BETSY Rawls
MARILYNN Smith
HOLLIS Stacy
JAN Stephenson
DONNA White
MICKEY Wright
BABE Zaharias

RAINY DAY COUNTRY CLUB IMPEDIMENTA

Unscramble the list and watch out for these hazards when you play.

1. rawet keslrpnir ______________________________
2. nwal wremo ______________________________
3. grof irah ______________________________
4. pli ______________________________
5. napor ______________________________
6. krae ______________________________
7. cenef ______________________________
8. urohg ______________________________
9. lusaca trawe ______________________________
10. krebnu ______________________________
11. tuo fo nubdso ______________________________
12. rnaabcar ______________________________
13. retes ______________________________
14. log ged ______________________________
15. skucd ______________________________
16. glaf sctik ______________________________
17. tovdi lohe ______________________________
18. dpon ______________________________
19. ngorud drenu erripa ______________________________
20. dhraazs ______________________________

RAINY DAY COUNTRY CLUB
FULL HANDICAP

Complete the words and post the letters.

1	2	3	4	5	6	7	8	9	10	11

12	13

14	15	16

1. Fore__addie
2. B__gey
3. A__ateur
4. Un__layable
5. W__dge
6. S__ymie
7. N__blick
8. Floa__er
9. Fr__nge
10. Appr__ach
11. Sha__k
12. Obstruct__on
13. Flag__tick
14. Li__t
15. P__tting
16. Fla__ge

THE RAINY DAY GOLFER'S "WHAT'S IN A NAME" TOURNAMENT

Complete the blanks using some or all of the last names.

1. Cut	Jack NICKlaus	a. George Archer
2. A male relative	______________	b. Seve Ballesteros
3. Cost	______________	c. Rex Caldwell
4. Objective	______________	d. Donna Caponi
5. Theatrical	______________	e. Jo Anne Carner
6. Relative	______________	f. Bob Goalby
7. User of bow and arrow	______________	g. Juli Inkster
8. Hand	______________	h. Larry Nelson
9. Sphere	______________	i. Jack Nicklaus
10. Hat	______________	j. Sandra Palmer
11. Feel good	______________	k. Gary Player
12. Auto	______________	l. Judy Rankin
13. Writing supply	______________	m. Kathy Whitworth

RAINY DAY COUNTRY CLUB EMBLEM

COLOR IN THE EMBLEM

• cut it out •

• paste it on cardboard •

PIN IT ON YOUR JACKET POCKET

ANSWERS

Page 1 MAZE

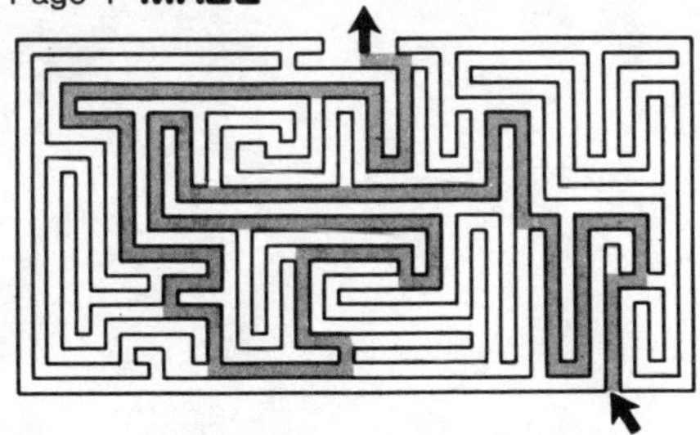

Page 2 CROSSWORD PUZZLE

Page 3 TWOSOME TOURNEY

1. Putter
2. Chipper
3. Spoon
4. Umbrella
5. Gimmie
6. Brassie
7. Whiff
8. Tee
9. Woods
10. Duffer
11. Green
12. Waggle
13. Hook
14. Callaway
15. Caddie
16. Ball
17. Grass
18. Baffy
19. Scuffing
20. Opponent
21. Handicapping
22. Naussau
23. Threesome
24. Gross

Page 4 LEADER BOARD

1. Lee Trevino
2. Ray Floyd
3. Gary Player
4. Nick Faldo
5. Hubie Green
6. Tom Kite
7. Arnold Palmer
8. Andy Bean
9. Cal Peete
10. Jack Nicklaus

Page 5 OTHER FAMOUS COURSES

1 - n	8 - j	15 - k
2 - o	9 - b	16 - m
3 - r	10 - f	17 - p
4 - s	11 - g	18 - l
5 - t	12 - h	19 - a
6 - e	13 - d	20 - c
7 - q	14 - i	

Page 6 WHAT'S IN A NAME, ROUND 1

1 - b, 2 - l, 3 - e, 4 - f, 5 - i, 6 - k, 7 - m, 8 - g, 9 - h, 10 - a, 11 - c, 12 - j, 13 - d

Page 7 MID-WEEK TOURNEY

out of bounds

1. pom poms
2. rubber cleats
3. towel
4. glove
5. plus fours
6. windbreaker
7. argyle socks
8. bermuda shorts
9. sun glasses
10. peaked cap
11. sweater

Page 8 HALL OF FAME

1 - n, 2 - f, 3 - q, 4 - l, 5 - s, 6 - j, 7 - r, 8 - p, 9 - a, 10 - m, 11 - i, 12 - b, 13 - c, 14 - e, 15 - k, 16 - d, 17 - o, 18 - g, 19 - h

Page 9 HIDING IN THE ROUGH

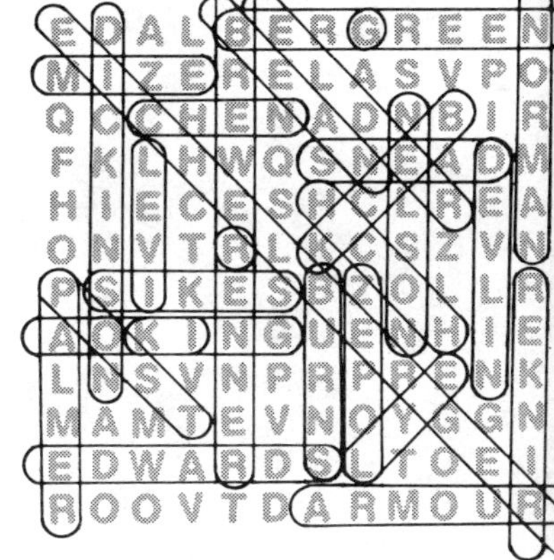

Page 10 OLD TIMERS SALE

1 - f, 2 - d, 3 - i, 4 - e, 5 - m , 6 - h, 7 - c, 8 - l, 9 - k, 10 - a, 11 - g,

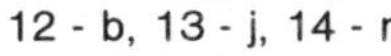
12 - b, 13 - j, 14 - n

Page 11 PARAPHERNALIA

1. rule book
2. divot repairer
3. suction cup
4. ginty
5. shag bag
6. range finder
7. sun tan lotion
8. score counter
9. steel brush
10. insect repellent
11. jacket
12. shoes
13. glove
14. putter
15. band-aid
16. chipper
17. hat
18. umbrella
19. ball marker
20. texas wedge
21. whiffle ball
22. head covers
23. clubs

Page 12 RDG WOULD RATHER PLAY GOLF

1 - k, 2 - g, 3 - j, 4 - r, 5 - p, 6 - h, 7 - n, 8 - s, 9 - c, 10 - a, 11 - q, 12 - e, 13 - f, 14 - i, 15 - l, 16 - m, 17 - d, 18 - o, 19 - b

Page 14 TRIVIA HANDICAP

1 - c, 2 - b, 3 - b, 4 - a, 5 - b, 6 - c, 7 - a, 8 - c, 9 - a

Page 15 PRO-AM

1. Alcott
2. Ford
3. Jones
4. Dickinson
5. Mayer
6. Watson
7. Graham
8. King
9. Simpson
10. Miller
11. Caldwell
12. Ahern
13. Sills
14. Wright
15. Colbert
16. Nelson
17. Young
18. Mudd
19. White
20. Stewart

Page 16 FUN

1.	D	ivot
2. sc	U	ff
3. out o	F	turn
4. whi	F	f
5. sp	E	ak
6. ma	R	kers
7.	S	hank

1.	G	love
2. b	O	gie
3. s	L	ice
4.	F	ore
5.	E	agle
6.	R	ough
7.	S	ink

Page 17 FIND THE SLEEVE

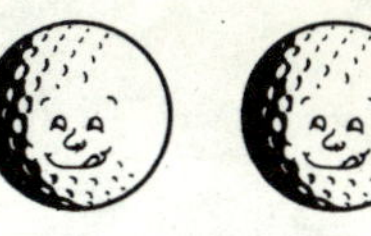

Page 18 SHOT GUN TOURNAMENT

Page 19 IMPEDIMENTA

1. water sprinkler
2. lawn mower
3. frog-hair
4. lip
5. apron
6. rake
7. fence
8. rough
9. casual water
10. bunker
11. out of bounds
12. barranca
13. trees
14. dog leg
15. ducks
16. flag stick
17. divot hole
18. pond
19. ground under repair
20. hazards

Page 20 FULL HANDICAP

Competition is fun

Page 21 WHAT'S IN A NAME, Round 2

1 - i, 2 - h, 3 - m, 4 - f, 5 - k, 6 - l, 7 - a, 8 - j, 9 - b, 10 - d, 11 - c, 12 - e, 13 - g

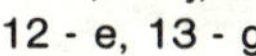

pss!®